Witty, Wicked, and Wise

A Book of Quotations About Women

Edited by Maureen Slattery

BARNES & NOBLE BOOKS

NEW YORK

Compilation copyright © 2003 by Barnes & Noble, Inc.

2003 Barnes & Noble Books

ISBN 0-7607-4730-x

Printed and bound in the United States of America

M 9 8 7 6 5 4 3 2

She's Always a Woman

One is not born, but rather, becomes, a woman.

—SIMONE DE BEAUVOIR

Despite my thirty years of research into the feminine soul, I have not been able to answer...the great question that has never been answered: "What does a woman want?"

—SIGMUND FREUD

A woman is like a tea bag. You never know how strong she is until she gets into hot water.

—ELEANOR ROOSEVELT

From women's eyes this doctrine I derive:
They sparkle still the right Promethean fire;
They are the books, the arts, the academes,
That show, contain, and nourish all the world.

—WILLIAM SHAKESPEARE, *Love's Labour's Lost*

In politics, if you want anything said, ask a man—
if you want anything done, ask a woman.

—MARGARET THATCHER

And a woman is only a woman, but a good cigar
is a smoke.

—RUDYARD KIPLING, *The Betrothed*

Women have no wilderness in them,
They are provident instead,
Content in the tight hot cell of their hearts
To eat dusty bread.

—LOUISE BOGAN, "Women"

Why are women...so much more interesting to men than men are to women?

—VIRGINIA WOOLF

Yeah, you know, boys, a nuclear reactor is a lot like a woman. You just have to read the manual and press the right buttons.

—HOMER J. SIMPSON, *The Simpsons*

She takes just like a woman, yes, she does
She makes love just like a woman, yes, she does
And she aches just like a woman
But she breaks just like a little girl.

> —BOB DYLAN, "Just Like A Woman"

For men at most differ as heaven and earth,
But women, worst and best, as heaven and hell.

> —ALFRED TENNYSON

A woman like that is not a woman, quite.
I have been her kind.

> —ANNE SEXTON, "Her Kind"

A thinking woman sleeps with monsters.
The beak that grips her, she becomes.

> —ADRIENNE RICH

Women in drudgery knew
They must be one of four:
Whores, artists, saints, and wives.
There are composite lives
that women always live.

—MURIEL RUKEYSER, "Wreath of Women"

Women forget all those things they don't want to remember, and remember everything they don't want to forget. The dream is the truth.

—ZORA NEALE HURSTON

she is sublimation
she is the essence of thee
she is concentrating on
he, who is chosen by she
here I go and I don't know why
I fell so ceaselessly
could it be he's taking over me...

—PATTI SMITH, "Dancing Barefoot"

All women are misfits, I think; we do not fit into this world without amputations.

—MARGE PIERCY, *Braided Lives*

Women are repeatedly accused of taking things personally. I cannot see any other honest way of taking them.

—MARYA MANNES

I've been on a calendar, but never on time.

—MARILYN MONROE

I'm the water I'm the dishes I'm the soap
I will comfort make you clean help you cope
When you're tired feeling helpless
Come inside I am the shelter
And then when you're feeling better
I'll watch you go.

—SLEATER-KINNEY, "Little Babies"

Women will love her, that she is a woman
More worth than any man; men, that she is
The rarest of all women.

     —WILLIAM SHAKESPEARE, *A Winter's Tale*

Women sometimes seem to share a quiet, unalter-
able dogma of persecution that endows even the
most sophisticated of them with the inarticulate
poignancy of the peasant.

     —ZELDA FITZGERALD

I'm wife; I've finished that,
That other state;
I'm Czar, I'm woman now:
It's safer so.

     —EMILY DICKINSON

Women are one of the Almighty's enigmas to prove
to men that He knows more than they do.

—ELLEN GLASGOW

Feisty Feminists

I do not believe that women are better than men. We have not wrecked railroads, nor corrupted legislature, nor done many unholy things that men have done; but then we must remember that we have not had the chance.

—JANE ADDAMS

It is easier to live through someone else than to become complete yourself.

—BETTY FRIEDAN

Living by proxy is always a precarious expedient.

—SIMONE DE BEAUVOIR

Now we are expected to be as wise as men who have had generations of all the help there is, and we scarcely anything.

—LOUISA MAY ALCOTT

I myself have never been able to find out precisely what feminism is. I only know that people call me a feminist whenever I express sentiments that differentiate me from a doormat or a prostitute.

—REBECCA WEST

A good part—and definitely the most fun part—of being a feminist is about frightening men.

—JULIE BURCHILL

I do not wish them to have power over men; but over themselves.

—MARY WOLLESTONECRAFT

I think being a woman is like being Irish.... Everyone says you're important and nice but you take second place all the same.

—IRIS MURDOCH, *The Red and The Green*

Women's degradation is in man's idea of his sexual rights. Our religion, laws, customs are all founded on the belief that woman was made for man.

—ELIZABETH CADY STANTON

It is narrow-minded in their more privileged fellow creatures to say that they ought to confine themselves to making puddings and knitting stockings, to playing on the piano and embroidering bags. It is thoughtless to condemn them, or laugh at them, if they seek to do more or learn more than custom has pronounced necessary for their sex.

—Charlotte Brontë

Women, we might as well be dogs baying the moon as petitioners without the right to vote!

—Susan B. Anthony

No woman can call herself free who does not own and control her body. No woman can call herself free until she can choose consciously whether she will or will not be a mother.

—Margaret Sanger

Had middle class black women begun a movement in which they had labeled themselves "oppressed," no one would have taken them seriously.

—BELL HOOKS

Women's rights is not only an abstraction, a cause; it is also a personal affair. It is not only about "us"; it is also about me and you. Just the two of us.

—TONI MORRISON

Women were fighting for limited freedom, the vote and more education. I wanted all the freedom, all the opportunity, all the equality there was in the world. I wanted to belong to the human race, not to a ladies' aid society to the human race.

—RHETA CHILDE DORR

Women have been taught that, for us, the earth is flat, and that if we venture out, we will fall off the edge. Some of us have ventured out nevertheless, and so far we have not fallen off.

—ANDREA DWORKIN

Women have a hard time of it in this world. They are oppressed by man-made laws, man-made social customs, masculine egoism, the delusion of masculine superiority. Their one comfort is the assurance that, even though it may be impossible to prevail against man, it is always possible to enslave and torture a man.

—H. L. MENCKEN

What do women want with votes, when they hold the sceptre of influence with which they can control even votes, if they wield it aright?

—MRS. H. O. WARD

"Feminine weakness" has generally meant that the female is more fragile and in general less strong than the male. But the fact is that the female is constitutionally stronger than the male and muscularly less powerful; she has greater stamina and lives longer.

—ASHLEY MONTAGU

Give women the vote, and in five years there will be a crushing tax on bachelors.

—GEORGE BERNARD SHAW

To conclude that women are unfitted to the task of our historic society seems to me the equivalent of closing male eyes to female facts.

—LYNDON B. JOHNSON

The idea of attaching one's self to a married woman, or of polishing one's manners to suit the standards of women of thirty, could hardly have entered the mind of a young Bostonian, and would have scandalised his parents. From women the boy got the domestic virtues and nothing else. He might not even catch the idea that women had more to give. The garden of Eden was hardly more primitive.

—HENRY ADAMS

The textile and needlework arts of the world, primarily because they have been the work of women have been especially written out of art history. It is a male idea that to be "high" and "fine" both women and art should be beautiful, but not useful or functional.

—PATRICIA MAINARDI, U.S. quilter

He travels fastest who travels alone, and that goes double for she. Real feminism is spinsterhood.

—FLORENCE KING

I'm a feminist, but I am liberating current feminism from these false feminists who have a death grip on it right now, who are antiporn and so on. I'm bringing, like Madonna, a sense of beauty and pleasure and sensuality back into feminism.

—CAMILLE PAGLIA

Sensible and responsible women do not want to vote. The relative positions to be assumed by man and woman in the working out of our civilization were assigned long ago by a higher intelligence than ours.

—GROVER CLEVELAND

There is one area in which I think Paglia and I would agree that politically correct feminism has produced a noticeable inequity. Nowadays, when a woman behaves in a hysterical and disagreeable fashion, we say, "Poor dear, it's probably PMS." Whereas, if a man behaves in a hysterical and disagreeable fashion, we say, "What an asshole." Let me leap to correct this unfairness by saying of Paglia, Sheesh, what an asshole.

—MOLLY IVINS

Women is losers
Women is losers
Women is losers, Lord, Lord, Lord, Lord!!!
So I know you must-a know, Lord,
Anywhere
Men almost seem to end up on top, oh!

—JANIS JOPLIN, "Women is Losers"

He Said, She Said

Sir, a woman preaching is like a dog's walking on his hind legs. It is not done well; but you are surprised to find it done at all.

—SAMUEL JOHNSON

Whatever women must do they must do twice as well as men to be thought half as good. Luckily, this is not difficult.

—CHARLOTTE WHITTON

God created woman. And boredom did indeed cease from that moment—but many other things ceased as well!

—FRIEDRICH W. NIETZSCHE

One of the things being in politics has taught is that men are not a reasoned or reasonable sex.

—MARGARET THATCHER

A woman of mystery is one who also has a certain maturity and whose actions speak louder than words. Any woman can be one, if she keeps those two points in mind. She should grow up—and shut up.

—ALFRED HITCHCOCK

I'm not denyin' the women are foolish; God Almighty made 'em to match the men.

—GEORGE ELIOT, *Adam Bede*

Jesus was a bachelor and never lived with a woman. Surely living with a woman is one of the most difficult things a man has to do, and he never did it.

—JAMES JOYCE

And verily, a woman need know but one man well, in order to understand all men; whereas a man may know all women and understand not one of them.

—HELEN ROWLAND

What a strange thing is man! and what a stranger
Is woman!

> —LORD BYRON, "Don Juan"

A woman will always sacrifice herself if you give her the opportunity. It is her favorite form of self-indulgence

> —W. SOMERSET MAUGHAM

Women want mediocre men, and men are working to be as mediocre as possible.

> —MARGARET MEAD

O woman, perfect woman! what distraction
Was meant to mankind when thou wast made
a devil!

> —JOHN FLETCHER

In passing, also, I would like to say that the first time Adam had a chance he laid the blame on a woman.

—LADY NANCY ASTOR

Women hate everything which strips off the tinsel of sentiment, and they are right, or it would rob them of their weapons.

—LORD BYRON

Let not women's weapons, water-drops,
Stain my man's cheeks!

—WILLIAM SHAKESPEARE, *King Lear*

The first thing that strikes the careless observer is that women are unlike men. They are "the opposite sex"—(though why "opposite" I do not know; what is the "neighboring sex"?)

—DOROTHY L. SAYERS

The quarrels of popes and kings, with wars and pestilences in every page; the men all so good for nothing, and hardly any women at all—it is very tiresome.

—Jane Austen

What mighty ills have not been done by woman!
Who was't betrayed the Capitol?—A woman!
Who lost Mark Antony the world?—A woman!
Who was the cause of a long ten years' war,
And laid at last old Troy in ashes?—Woman!
Destructive, damnable, deceitful woman!

—Thomas Otway, *The Orphan*

In a capitalist society a man is expected to be an aggressive, uncompromising, factual, lusty, intelligent provider of goods, and the woman, a retiring, gracious, emotional, intuitive, attractive consumer of goods.

—Toni Cade Bambara

Women have their heads in their hearts. Man seems to have been destined for a superior being; as things are, I think women generally better creatures than men. They have weaker appetites and weaker intellects but much stronger affections. A man with a bad heart has been sometimes saved by a strong head; but a corrupt woman is lost forever.

—SAMUEL TAYLOR COLERIDGE

Women are all the bloody same...you can't love for five minutes without wanting it abolished in brats and house bloody wifery.

—SAMUEL BECKETT, *Murphy*

Women have served all these centuries as looking-glasses possessing the magic and delicious power of reflecting the figure of man at twice its natural size.

—VIRGINIA WOOLF

Women love us for our defects. If we have enough of them, they will forgive us everything, even our gigantic intellects.

—Oscar Wilde

If men can run the world, why can't they stop wearing neckties? How intelligent is it to start the day by tying a noose around your neck?

—Linda Ellerbee

A man's women folk, whatever their outward show of respect for his merit and authority, always regard him secretly as an ass.

—H. L. Mencken

The women, who had congregated in the groves, set up the most violent clamors, as they invariably do here as elsewhere on every occasion of excitement and alarm, with a view of tranquilizing their own minds and disturbing other people.

—HERMAN MELVILLE, *Typee*

It's not as if we just insult women. Our insults go across the board

—MIKE D. (The Beastie Boys)

Can you imagine a world without men? No crime and lots of happy, fat women.

—NICOLE HOLLANDER

Let the men do their duty & the women will be such wonders, the female life lives from the light of the male.

—William Blake

A woman should be good for everything at home, but abroad good for nothing.

—Euripides

I hate women because they always know where things are.

—Voltaire

Whether women are better than men I cannot say, but I can say they are certainly no worse.

—Golda Meir

Being a woman is a terribly difficult task, since it consists principally in dealing with men.

—JOSEPH CONRAD

Women, can't live with them, can't live without them.

—DESIDERIUS ERASMUS

Most women set out to change a man, and when they have changed him they do not like him.

—MARLENE DIETRICH

If I were a girl, I'd despair. The supply of good women far exceeds that of the men who deserve them.

—ROBERT GRAVES

Sometimes it's hard to be a woman
Giving all your love to just one man
You'll have bad times
And he'll have good times.

        —TAMMY WYNETTE, "Stand By Your Man"

Wise Words from Women Who Know

Take your work seriously, but never yourself.

—Margot Fonteyn

One never notices what has been done; one can only see what remains to be done.

—Marie Curie

A mistake in judgment isn't fatal, but too much anxiety about judgment is.

—Pauline Kael

We still think of a powerful man as a born leader and a powerful woman as an anomaly.

—MARGARET ATWOOD

Everybody knows if you are too careful you are so occupied in being careful that you are sure to stumble over something.

—GERTRUDE STEIN

Life is either always a tight-rope or a feather bed. Give me the tight-rope.

—EDITH WHARTON

I don't think necessity is the mother of invention. Invention, in my opinion, arises directly from idleness, possibly also from laziness, to save oneself trouble.

—AGATHA CHRISTIE

If you have enough butter, anything is good.

—JULIA CHILD

Until you lose your reputation, you never realize what a burden it was or what freedom really is.

—MARGARET MITCHELL

If you obey all the rules, you miss all the fun.

—KATHARINE HEPBURN

Everyone has talent. What is rare is the courage to follow talent to the dark place where it leads.

—ERICA JONG

Creative minds have always been known to survive any kind of bad training.

—ANNA FREUD

Because I am a woman, I must make unusual efforts to succeed. If I fail, no one will say, "She doesn't have what it takes"; They will say, "Women don't have what it takes."

—CLARE BOOTHE LUCE

Be bold. If you're going to make an error, make a doozey, and don't be afraid to hit the ball.

—BILLIE JEAN KING

Life is either a daring adventure or nothing at all. Security is mostly a superstition. It does not exist in nature.

—HELEN KELLER

Success didn't spoil me, I've always been insufferable.

—FRAN LEBOWITZ

Seize the moment. Remember all those women on the *Titanic* who waved off the dessert cart.

—ERMA BOMBECK

Cautious, careful people, always casting about to preserve their reputation and social standing, never can bring about a reform. Those who are really in earnest must be willing to be anything or nothing in the world's estimation.

—SUSAN B. ANTHONY

I was elected by the women of Ireland, who instead of rocking the cradle, rocked the system.

—MARY ROBINSON, President of Ireland

Never think you've seen the last of anything.

—EUDORA WELTY

I'm not a pitiable creature. It's just that I suffer very eloquently.

—JONI MITCHELL

The Fathers of Culture get anxious about paternity. They start talking about legitimacy.... This involves intellectual abortion by centuries of women artists, infanticide of works by women writers, and a whole medical corps of sterilizing critics working to purify the Canon, to reduce the subject matter and style of literature to something Ernest Hemingway could have understood.

—URSULA LE GUIN

The cure for boredom is curiosity. There is no cure for curiosity.

—DOROTHY PARKER

Wicked Women

Only good girls keep diaries. Bad girls don't have time.

—TALLULAH BANKHEAD

Heaven has no rage like love to hatred turned,
Nor hell a fury like a woman scorned.

—WILLIAM CONGREVE

In revenge and in love woman is more barbarous than man.

—FRIEDRICH W. NIETZCHE

Virtue has its own reward, but has no sale at the box office.

—MAE WEST

You been around enough to know
That if I want to leave you better let me go
Because I take full advantage
Of every man I meet
I get away almost every day
With what the girls call...
The girls call murder.

—LIZ PHAIR, "Girls! Girls! Girls!"

Women is fine once you got 'em pinned down, boss, but when they ain't pinned down they're hell.

—JOHN DOS PASSOS

Then said he, "Wife, now that you are Pope, be satisfied, you cannot become anything greater now." "I will consider about that," said the woman. Thereupon they both went to bed, but she was not satisfied, and greediness let her have no sleep, for she was continually thinking what there was left for her to be.

—BROTHERS GRIMM, "The Fisherman and his Wife"

Good girls go to heaven, bad girls go everywhere.

—HELEN GURLEY BROWN

Women have no sympathy...and my experience of women is almost as large as Europe.

—FLORENCE NIGHTINGALE

JOHNNY CLAY: You like money. You got a great big dollar sign there where most women have a heart. So play it smart. Stay in character and you'll have money. Plenty of it. George'll have it and he'll blow it on you. Probably buy himself a five-cent cigar.

SHERRY PEATTY: You don't know me very well, Johnny. I wouldn't think of letting George throw his money away on cigars.

—STANLEY KUBRICK, *The Killing*

If a woman hasn't got a tiny streak of harlot in her, she is a dry stick as a rule.

—D. H. LAWRENCE

Beautiful women, whose beauty meant more than it said…was their brilliancy always fed by something coarse and concealed? Was that their secret?

—WILLA CATHER

Such is my jealousy
(that I discreetly veil
with just my smile)
that I would clear so fiery a space
that no mere woman's love could long endure.

—HILDA DOOLITTLE (H.D.), "Red Roses for Bronze"

The women who inspired this play deserved to be smacked across the head with a meat ax and that, I flatter myself, is exactly what I smacked them with.

—CLARE BOOTHE LUCE

There is in every true woman's heart, a spark of heavenly fire, which lies dormant in the broad daylight of prosperity, but which kindles up and beams and blazes in the dark hour of adversity.

—WASHINGTON IRVING

The reason good women like me and flock to my pictures is that there is a little bit of vampire instinct in every woman.

—THEDA BARA

With attractive women…juries sometimes have to be restrained from handing them a medal for their crimes.

—JOHN MCGEORGE, Australian psychiatrist

Most women defend themselves. It is the female of the species—it is the tigress and lioness in you—which tends to defend when attacked.

—MARGARET THATCHER

I expect Woman will be the last thing civilized by Man.

—GEORGE MEREDITH

Having no apparatus except gut fear and female cunning to examine this formless magic, to understand how it works, how to measure its field strength, count its lines of force, she may fall back on superstition, or take up a useful hobby like embroidery, or go mad, or marry a disc jockey.

—THOMAS PYNCHON, *The Crying of Lot 49*

Men, some to business, some to pleasure take;
But every woman is at heart a rake.

—ALEXANDER POPE

When women go wrong, men go right after them.

—MAE WEST

On Mars there are no women

—PERE UBU, "Red Sky," lyrics by David Thomas

UNCLE CHARLIE: The cities are full of women, middle-aged widows, husbands dead, husbands who've spent their lives making fortunes, working and working. And then they die and leave their money to their wives, their silly wives. And what do the wives do, these useless women? You see them in the hotels, the best hotels, every day by the thousands. Drinking the money, eating the money, losing the money at bridge. Playing all day and all night. Smelling of money. Proud of their jewelry but of nothing else. Horrible. Faded, fat, greedy women.

—THORTON WILDER, *Shadow of a Doubt*

The two women exchanged the kind of glance women use when no knife is handy.

—ELLERY QUEEN

Women are natural guerillas. Scheming, we nestle into the enemy's bed, avoiding open warfare, watching the options, playing the odds.

—SALLY KEMPTON

A pessimist is a man who thinks all women are bad. An optimist is one who hopes they are.

—CHAUNCEY DEPEW

Women's virtue is man's greatest invention.

—CORNELIA OTIS SKINNER

Lead me not into temptation; I can find the way myself.

—RITA MAE BROWN

A woman can look both moral and exciting, if she also looks as if it was quite a struggle.

—EDNA FERBER

If I had to give a definition of capitalism I would say: the process whereby American girls turn into American women.

—CHRISTOPHER HAMPTON

She even had a kind of special position among men: she was an exception, she fitted none of the categories they commonly used when talking about girls; she wasn't a cock-teaser, a cold fish, an easy lay or a snarky bitch; she was an honorary person. She had grown to share their contempt for most women.

—MARGARET ATWOOD, "The Man from Mars"

The Wittier Sex

If you haven't got anything nice to say about any-
body, come sit next to me.

—attributed to ALICE LONGWORTH

One cannot be always laughing at a man without
now and then stumbling on something witty.

—JANE AUSTEN

Women would rather be right than reasonable.

—OGDEN NASH

They say that women talk too much. If you have worked in congress you know that the filibuster was invented by men.

—CLARE BOOTHE LUCE

Women speak because they wish to speak, whereas a man speaks only when driven to speech by something outside himself—like, for instance, he can't find any clean socks.

—JEAN KERR

The silliest woman can manage a clever man; but it needs a very clever woman to manage a fool!

—RUDYARD KIPLING

A witty woman is a treasure; a witty beauty is a power.

—GEORGE MEREDITH

The real offense, as she ultimately perceived, was her having a mind of her own at all. Her mind was to be his—attached to his own like a small garden plot to a deer park.

—HENRY JAMES, *The Portrait of a Lady*

Hypocrite women, how seldom we speak
of our own doubts, while dubiously
we mother man in his doubt!

—DENISE LEVERTOV, "Hypocrite Women"

It's an indulgence to sit in a room and discuss your beliefs as if they were a juicy piece of gossip.

—LILLIAN HELLMAN

I'll not listen to reason. Reason always means what someone else has got to say.

—ELIZABETH CLEGHORN GASKELL

The people I'm furious with are the women's liberationists. They keep getting up on soapboxes and proclaiming women are brighter than men. That's true, but it should be kept quiet or it ruins the whole racket.

—ANITA LOOS

Man forgives woman anything save the wit to outwit him.

—MINNA ANTRIM

The witty woman is a tragic figure in American life. Wit destroys eroticism and eroticism destroys wit, so women must choose between taking lovers and taking no prisoners.

—FLORENCE KING

A respectable tea-party merely—whose gossip would be Universal History. The fourth old woman from myself suckled Columbus—the ninth was nurse to the Norman Conqueror—the nineteenth was the Virgin Mary—the twenty-fourth was the Cum'an Sibyl—the thirtieth was at the Trojan war and Helen her name—the thirty-eighth was Queen Semiramis—the sixtieth was Eve, the mother of mankind. So much for the "Old woman that lives under the hill, And if she's not gone she lives there still."

—HENRY DAVID THOREAU

Uneducated clever women, who have seen much of the world, are in middle life so much the most cultured part of the community. They have been saved from this horrible burden of inert ideas.

—ALFRED NORTH WHITEHEAD

Of course we women gossip on occasion. But our appetite for it is not as avid as a man's. It is in the boys' gyms, the college fraternity houses, the club locker rooms, the paneled offices of business that gossip reaches its luxuriant flower.

—PHYLLIS MCGINLEY

They call women the weakest vessel but I think they are the Strongest. A girl has always more tongue than a boy I have seen a little brat no higher than a nettle & she had as much tongue as a city clark...

—WILLIAM BLAKE

E'en silly women have defensive arts,
Their eyes, their tongues—and nameless other parts.

—ROBERT BURNS, "A Poem in Embryo"

The Most
Beautiful Girl...

We poets would die of loneliness but for women,
and we choose our men friends that we may have
somebody to talk about women with.

—W. B. YEATS

Round and round, like a dance of snow
In a dazzling drift, as its guardians, go
Floating the women faded for ages,
Sculptured in stone on the poet's pages.

—ROBERT BROWNING, "Women and Roses"

You women could make someone fall in love even with a lie.

—GEORG BCHNER

Some women, when they kiss, blush, some call the cops, some swear, some bite, some laugh, some cry. Me? I die. Die. I die inside when you kiss me.

—SAM FULLER, *Underworld, U.S.A.*

Women are systematically degraded by receiving the trivial attentions which men think it manly to pay to the sex, when, in fact, men are insultingly supporting their own superiority.

—MARY WOLLSTONECRAFT

'Tisn't beauty, so to speak, nor good talk necessarily. It's just IT. Some women'll stay in a man's memory if they once walked down a street.

—RUDYARD KIPLING

What, when drunk, one sees in other women, one sees in Garbo sober.

—KENNETH TYNAN

In my ballets, woman is first. Men are consorts. God made men to sing the praises of women. They are not equal to men: They are better.

—GEORGE BALANCHINE

In Hollywood, the women are all peaches. It makes one long for an apple occasionally.

—W. SOMERSET MAUGHM

If the Lord made anything better than a woman, he kept it for Himself.

—JERRY LEE LEWIS

The sensation of seeing extremely fine women, with superb forms, perfectly unconscious of undress, and yet evidently aware of their beauty and dignity, is worth a week's seasickness to experience

—HENRY ADAMS

Oh, a pretty girl is like a violent crime
If you do it wrong you could do time
But if you do it right it is sublime.

—MAGNETIC FIELDS, "A Pretty Girl is Like...,"
lyrics by Stephin Merritt

All women are wonders because they reduce all men to the obvious.

—GEOFFREY HOMES, *Out of the Past*

I, I love the colorful clothes she wears
And the way the sunlight plays upon her hair
I hear the sound of a gentle word
On the wind that lifts her perfume through the air.

—BEACH BOYS, "Good Vibrations,"
written by Brian Wilson and Mike Love

If women didn't exist, all the money in the world would have no meaning.

—ARISTOTLE ONASSIS

Anyone who says he can see through women is missing a lot.

—GROUCHO MARX

Then from amaze into delight he fell
To hear her whisper woman's lore so well;
And every word she spake entic'd him on
To unperplex'd delight and pleasure known.

—JOHN KEATS, "Lamia"

Of all the paths [that] lead to a woman's love
Pity 's the straightest.

—BEAUMONT AND FLETCHER, *The Knight of Malta*

The fickleness of the women I love is only equaled by the infernal consistency of the women who love me.

—GEORGE BERNARD SHAW

Why should I paint dead fish, onions and beer glasses? Girls are so much prettier.

—MARIE LAURENCIN

I was about half in love with her by the time we sat down. That's the thing about girls. Every time they do something pretty...you fall half in love with them, and then you never know where the hell you are.

—J. D. Salinger

Women are really much nicer than men: No wonder we like them.

—Kingsley Amis

Then sing as Martin Luther sang,
As Doctor Martin Luther sang,
"Who loves not wine, woman and song,
He is a fool his whole life long."

—William Makepeace Thackery

How can a woman be expected to be happy with a man who insists on treating her as if she were a perfectly normal human being.

—OSCAR WILDE

The ideal woman which is in every man's mind is evoked by a word or phrase or the shape of her wrist, her hand. The most beautiful description of a woman is by understatement. Remember, all Tolstoy ever said to describe Anna Karenina was that she was beautiful and could see in the dark like a cat.

—WILLIAM FAULKNER

Welcome to the Working Week

Tailor's work—the finishing of men's outside gar-
ments—was the "trade" learned most frequently by
women in [the 1820s and 1830s], and one or more
of my older sisters worked at it; I think it must have
been at home, for I somehow or somewhere got
the idea, while I was a small child, that the chief
end of woman was to make clothing for mankind.

—LUCY LARCOM

All my life, I always wanted to be somebody. Now I see that I should have been more specific.

—attributed to LILY TOMLIN

You are your work. Don't trade the stuff of your life, time, for nothing more than dollars. That's a rotten bargain.

—RITA MAE BROWN

My grandfather once told me that there were two kinds of people: those who do the work and those who take the credit. He told me to try to be in the first group. There was much less competition.

—INDIRA GANDHI

I have yet to hear a man ask for advice on how to combine marriage and a career.

—GLORIA STEINEM

It's people like me who have careers who really have bitched up the old relationship between men and women. Women ought to be soft and gentle and dependent. Disembodied spirits like myself are all wrong.

—DAPHNE DU MAURIER

Women think that an engineer is a man in hip boots building a dam. They don't realize that 95 percent of engineering is done in a nice air-conditioned office.

—BEATRICE ALICE HICKS

Everyone knew in the 1950s why a girl from a nice family left home. The meaning of her theft of herself from her parents was clear to all—as well as what she'd been up to in the room of her own.

—JOYCE JOHNSON, *Minor Characters*

I suppose I could have stayed home and baked cookies and had teas.

—HILLARY RODHAM CLINTON

In a world where there is so much to be done, I felt strongly impressed that there must be something for me to do.

—DOROTHEA DIX

In a world where women work three times as hard for half as much, our achievement has been denigrated, both marriage and divorce have turned against us, our motherhood has been used as an obstacle to our success, our passion as a trap, our empathy for others as an excuse to underpay us.

—ERICA JONG

I am not a suffragist, nor do I believe in "careers" for women, especially a "career" in factory and mill where most working women have their "careers." A great responsibility rests upon woman—the training of children. This is her most beautiful task.

—MOTHER JONES

People assume you slept your way to the top. Frankly, I couldn't sleep my way to the middle.

—JONI EVANS

I believe that it is as much a right and duty for women to do something with their lives as for men and we are not going to be satisfied with such frivolous parts as you give us.

—LOUISA MAY ALCOTT

The characteristics most highly developed in women and perhaps most essential to human beings are the very characteristics that are specifically dysfunctional for success in the world as it is.... They may, however, be the important ones for making the world different.

—JEAN BAKER MILLER

Housekeeping is not beautiful; it cheers and raises neither the husband, the wife, nor the child; neither the host nor the guest; it oppresses women. A house kept to the end of prudence is laborious without joy; a house kept to the end of display is impossible to all but a few women, and their success is dearly bought.

—RALPH WALDO EMERSON

I think housework is the reason most women go to the office.

—HELOISE CRUSE

The domestic career is no more natural to all women than the military career is natural to all men.

—GEORGE BERNARD SHAW

Housework can't kill you, but why take a chance?

—PHYLLIS DILLER

I agree today that a man has no business trying to tell women what their characteristics are, which ones are inborn, which are more admirable, which will be best utilized by what occupations.

—BENJAMIN SPOCK

I said that if people tell you your mother is not prime minister anymore, you just turn around and say, "So what? How often has your mother been prime minister?"

—BENAZIR BHUTTO to her children

Q: What would have made a family and career
easier for you?
A: Being born a man.

—ANONYMOUS

Body and Soul

If God had wanted us to think with our wombs, why did he give us a brain?

—CLARE BOOTH LUCE

Women complain about premenstrual syndrome, but I think of it as the only time of the month that I can be myself.

—ROSEANNE BARR

Women of the tradition to which Alice and Martha belonged are prepared to discuss menstruation or pregnancy in the frankest of detail, but it is taboo to discuss sex.

—DORIS LESSING, *A Proper Marriage*

I didn't know how babies were made until I was pregnant with my fourth child.

—LORETTA LYNN

If pregnancy were a book, they would cut the last two chapters.

—NORA EPHRON

Pregnancy is of course confined to women, but it is in other ways significantly different from the typical covered disease or disability.

—WILLIAM H. REHNQUIST

Whoever thought up the word "Mammogram"? Every time I hear it, I think I'm supposed to put my breast in an envelope and send it to someone.

—JAN KING

God gave women intuition and femininity. Used properly, the combination easily jumbles the brain of any man I've ever met.

—FARRAH FAWCETT

If high heels were so wonderful, men would still be wearing them.

—SUE GRAFTON

I'm not offended by all the dumb blonde jokes because I know I'm not dumb and I'm also not blonde.

—DOLLY PARTON

I never go out unless I look like Joan Crawford the movie star. If you want to see the girl next door, go next door.

—JOAN CRAWFORD

A girl with brains ought to do something else with them besides think.

—ANITA LOOS

Women are not supposed to have uteruses, especially in poems.

—MAXINE KUMIN

I have a brain and a uterus, and I use both.

—PATRICIA SCHROEDER

Women have face-lifts in a society in which women without them appear to vanish from sight.

—Naomi Wolf

And how many women really lovely and good—especially good—commit esthetic suicide by letting themselves slide down to where they "feel natural" in an old gray flannel wrapper, not only actually but mentally.

—Emily Post

Music play make me dreamy for dancing
Must be a way that I can dress to please him
It's hard to walk and the dress is not easy
I'm swinging over like a heavy loaded fruit tree.

—P. J. Harvey, "Dress"

Men make clothes for the women they'd like to be with or—in most cases—the women they'd like to be.

—ROBERT ALTMAN, *Prêt a Porter*

A woman's dress should be like a barbed-wire fence: serving its purpose without obstructing the view.

—SOPHIA LOREN

Look for the woman in the dress. If there is no woman, there is no dress.

—COCO CHANEL

It is better to be looked over than overlooked.

—MAE WEST

Television excites me because it seems to be the last stamping ground of poetry, the last place where I hear women's hair rhapsodically described, women's faces acclaimed in odelike language.

—BEN HECHT

I'm tired of all this nonsense about beauty being only skin-deep. That's deep enough. What do you want—an adorable pancreas?

—JEAN KERR

Every day, in every way, the billion-dollar beauty business tells women they are monsters in disguise…women are told they are the fair sex, but at the same time that their "beauty" needs lifting, shaping, dyeing, painting, curling, padding. Women are really being told that "the beauty" is a beast.

—UNA STANNARD

Few girls are as well shaped as a good horse.

—HANNAH ARENDT

Sometimes straight men freak out when I talk about my period. I don't talk about it that much considering how much it happens—I barely mention it. But I guarantee if straight men had a period, you would never hear the end of it. They would be using old socks, coffee filters.... Every bachelor apartment would look like a murder scene.

—MARGARET CHO

A male gynecologist is like an auto mechanic who never owned a car.

—CARRIE SNOW

Don't you realize that as long as you have to sit down to pee, you'll never be a dominant force in the world? You'll never be a convincing techno-crat or middle manager. Because people will know. She's in there sitting down.

—DON DELILLO, *The Names*

All the American women had purple noses and gray lips and their faces were chalk white from terrible powder. I recognized that the United States could be my life's work.

—HELENA RUBINSTEIN

I'm a big woman. I need big hair.

—ARETHA FRANKLIN

The two greatest mannequins of the century were Gertrude Stein and Edith Sitwell—unquestionably. You just couldn't take a bad picture of those two old girls.

—DIANA VREELAND

Marriage and Motherhood

A women without a man cannot meet a man, any man, of any age, without thinking, even if it's for a half-second, Perhaps this is *the* man.

—DORIS LESSING, *The Golden Notebook*

A living doll, everywhere you look.
It can sew, it can cook,
It can talk, talk, talk....
My boy, it's your last resort.
Will you marry it, marry it, marry it.

—SYLVIA PLATH, "The Applicant"

Given the expectations of society at large, men are generally correct in their assumption that it is important for a woman to have a man. What they do not understand is how pathetically little difference it makes WHAT man.

—GLORIA STEINEM

As she made the beds, shopped for groceries, matched slipcover material, ate peanut butter sandwiches with her children, chauffeured up Scouts and Brownies, lay beside her husband at night—she was afraid to ask even of herself the silent question—"Is this all?"

—BETTY FRIEDAN

The trouble with some women is they get all excited about nothing—and then they marry him.

—CHER

She rose to his requirement, dropped
The playthings of her life
To take the honorable work
Of woman and of wife.

—EMILY DICKINSON

The Law has made the man and wife one person,
and that one person the husband!

—LUCRETIA MOTT

Love, the strongest and deepest element in all
life, the harbinger of hope, of joy, of ecstasy; love,
the defier of all laws, of all conventions; love,
the freest, the most powerful molder of human
destiny; how can such an all-compelling force
be synonymous with that poor little State-and
Church-begotten weed, marriage?

—EMMA GOLDMAN

A man loves a woman so much, he asks her to marry—to change her name, quit her job, have and raise his babies, be home when gets there, move where his job is. You can hardly imagine what he might ask if he didn't love her.

—GABRIELLE BURTON

I've been married to one Marxist and one fascist, and neither one would take the garbage out.

—LEE GRANT

A girl must marry for love and keep on marrying until she finds it.

—ZSA ZSA GABOR

Women hope men will change after marriage but they don't; men hope women won't change but they do.

—BETTINA ARNDT

Women—one half the human race at least—care fifty times more for a marriage than a ministry.

—WALTER BAGEHOT

Some women marry houses.
It's another kind of skin; it has a heart,
a mouth, a liver and bowel movements.

—ANNE SEXTON, "Housewife"

Do not put such unlimited power into the hands of the husbands. Remember all men would be tyrants if they could.

—ABIGAIL ADAMS

Marriage is for women the commonest mode of livelihood, and the total amount of undesired sex endured by women is probably greater in marriage than in prostitution.

—BERTRAND RUSSELL

All women become like their mothers. That is their tragedy. No man does. That's his.

—OSCAR WILDE

Of all movements of inertia, maternity and reproduction are the most typical, and women's property of moving in a constant line forever is ultimate, uniting history in its only unbroken and unbreakable sequence. Whatever else stops, the woman must go on reproducing.... If the laws of inertia are to be sought anywhere with certainty, it is in the feminine mind.

—HENRY ADAMS

Young women especially have something invested in being nice people, and it's only when you have children that you realise you're not a nice person at all, but generally a selfish bully.

—FAY WELDON

Take motherhood: nobody ever thought of putting it on a moral pedestal until some brash feminists pointed out, about a century ago, that the pay is lousy and the career ladder nonexistent.

—BARBARA EHRENREICH

Motherhood is the strangest thing, it can be like being one's own Trojan horse.

—REBECCA WEST

With what a price we pay for the glory of motherhood.

—ISADORA DUNCAN

Why do grandparents and grandchildren get along so well? They have the same enemy: the mother.

—CLAUDETTE COLBERT

Mother,
strange goddess face
above my milk home,
that delicate asylum,
I ate you up.

—ANNE SEXTON, "Dreaming the Breasts"

A mother! What are we worth really? They all grow up whether you look after them or not.

—CHRISTINA STEAD

It will be a pity if women in the more conventional mould are to be phased out, for there will never be anyone to go home to.

—ANITA BROOKNER, *A Friend from England*

Clearly, society has a tremendous stake in insisting on a woman's natural fitness for the career of mother: the alternatives are too expensive.

—ANN OAKLEY

GENERAL MCLAIDLAW: Lena will never marry. She's not the marrying sort. I see no reason to worry. There's enough to care for her for the rest of her life.

MRS. MCLAIDLAW: I suppose you're right, dear. I'm afraid she is rather spinsterish.

GENERAL MCLAIDLAW: What's wrong with that. The old maid's a respectable institution. All women are not alike. Lena has intellect and a fine solid character.

—SAMSON RAPHAELSON, *Suspicion*

Bachelors know more about women than married men; if they didn't they'd be married too.

—H. L. MENCKEN

Old maids, having never bent their temper or their lives to other lives and other tempers, as woman's destiny requires, have for the most part a mania for making everything about them bend to them.

—Honoré de Balzac

Bride: A woman with a fine prospect of happiness behind her.

—Ambrose Bierce

Never Ask A Woman Her Age

A woman can keep one secret—the secret of her age.

—Voltaire

Few women, I fear, have had such reason as I have to think the long sad years of youth were worth living for the sake of middle age.

—Dwight D. Eisenhower

A woman's always younger than a man of equal years.

—Elizabeth Barrett Browning

Who would ever think that so much went on in the soul of a young girl?

—Anne Frank

A grown woman should not have to masquerade as a girl in order to remain in the land of the living.

—Germaine Greer

At fifteen, beauty and talent do not exist; there can only be promise of the coming woman.

—Honoré de Balzac

Like many women my age, I am 28 years old.

—MARY SCHMICH

Age is something that doesn't matter, unless you are a cheese.

—BILLIE BURKE

The women cry,
Come, my fox,
heal me.
I am chalk white
with middle age
so wear me threadbare. . . .

—ANNE SEXTON, "The Little Peasant"

The really frightening thing about middle age is the knowledge that you'll grow out of it.

—DORIS DAY

The hardest years in life are those between ten and seventy.

—HELEN HAYES

She was a handsome woman of forty-five and would remain so for many years.

—ANITA BROOKNER

Inside every older person is a younger person—wondering what the hell happened.

—CORA HARVEY ARMSTRONG

One's prime is elusive. You little girls, when you grow up, must be on the alert to recognize your prime at whatever time of your life it may occur.

—MURIEL SPARK, *The Prime of Miss Jane Brodie*

The older one grows, the more one likes indecency.

—Virginia Woolf

Old age is no place for sissies.

—Bette Davis

A woman would rather visit her own grave than the place where she has been young and beautiful after she is aged and ugly.

—Thomas Hardy

There's no such thing as old age, there is only sorrow.

—Edith Wharton

What a wonderful life I've had! I only wish I'd realized it sooner.

—COLLETTE

Let the athlete die young and laurel-crowned. Let the soldiers earn the Purple Hearts. Let women die old, white-crowned, with human hearts.

—URSULA LE GUIN

It is not true that life is one damn thing after another. It's one damn thing over and over.

—EDNA ST. VINCENT MILLAY

Life is hard—after all, it kills you.

—KATHERINE HEPBURN